Distractions

that keep us from being who we are
& doing what we really want to do

Faith Strong

© 2005 by Faith Strong

"But Beautiful," page 13, from the love song written by James Van Heusen and Johnny Burke, A.S.C.A.P.

"I Am Not I," page 39, reprinted from *Lorca and Jimenez: Selected Poems,* chosen and translated by Robert Bly, Beacon Press, Boston, 1997. © 1997 Robert Bly. Used with his permission.

"I lived on the shady side of the road...," page 55, reprinted with the permission of Simon & Schuster, Inc., from THE COLLECTED POEMS AND PLAYS OF RABINDRANATH TAGORE by Rabindranath Tagore. Copyright © 1937 by The Macmillan Company.

To order more copies of this book or to communicate with the author:
faithf.strong@comcast.net

THIRD PRINTING

ISBN 0-9718681-0-7

Designed by Graphic Solutions Inc-Chicago
This book is printed on acid-free paper

An Opening

I will never forget the great teacher, Krishnamurti, yelling at us, "When are you going to get serious about your life?" This was a contradiction to the words I'd heard all my life: "Don't take yourself so seriously."

I have made peace with this seeming contradiction by realizing that being serious can mean wallowing in the past—regrets, guilt, mistakes, blame, grief—for eons of time putting my life on hold! And getting serious about my life is in knowing it's up to me to choose to love it—to grow and to learn. So today I say:

"I don't take myself too seriously and I am serious about my life."

"Distractions" (that keep us from being who we are and doing what we really want to do) is a subject as deep as the ocean and as high as the sky—and even beyond that! But since I believe that less is often more, I like a brevity of words. So I encourage you to read this small book slowly. Pause and ponder after each sentence to absorb the meaning, the truth for you. Take the time to do the worksheets. It is a chance to slow down, to give yourself time to get the "Ah, Ha's."

My purpose is to have the words that have come through me improve both your life and mine. My intention is to take some of the hard work out of our lives, lessening the struggle we seem so attached to.

Let us awaken to living our lives in awe, in discovery, with a sweeter appreciation of others and ourselves.

I dedicate this book
to the creative genius
within each of us.

Contents

first things first...

Distractions 8

Who We Are 10

Doing What We Really Want to Do 12

Paradoxes 13

distractions...

1. **Comparing** 16
   Worksheet 19

2. **Excuses** 20
   Worksheet 24

3. **Procrastinating** 25
   Worksheet 27

4. **Complaining (and Blaming)** 28
   Worksheet 31

5. **Addictions/Habits** 32
   Worksheet 35

6. **Bigotries** 36
   I Am Not I (poem) 38
   Worksheet 39

7. **Minding Their Business** 40
   Worksheet 42

Time Out 43

I think continually.... (poem) 45

8. **Boredom** 46
   Worksheet 49

9. **Apathy** 50
   This is the true joy in life (poem) 51
   Worksheet 52

10. **Insecurities/Fear** 53
    I lived on the shady side... (poem) 55
    Worksheet 56

11. **Beliefs/Opinions** 57
    Worksheet 60

12. **Disorder** 61
    Worksheet 66

13. **Traditions** 67
    Worksheet 69

14. **Toxic Influence** 70
    Worksheet 73

15. **Irresponsibility** 74
    All That Is (poem) 78
    Worksheet 79

16. **Being Immovable** 80
    Immovable (poem) 81
    Worksheet 82

17. **Expectations/Hope** 83
    Worksheet 86

18. **Low Self Worth** 87
    Worksheet 90

onward...

Onward and Upward 92

Postscript 94

The Day our Skies Were Quiet (poem) 95

Acknowledgements 96

first things first . . .

Distractions

Webster defines *distract:* "to draw or cause to turn away from a goal, purpose, direction, association or interest," and *distraction* as a "diversion of the attention." For our purposes, I define distractions as something we create that keeps us from taking responsibility for our choices, our dreams, our creativity—our very lives if you will! We create them consciously and unconsciously. They are actions that have us taking another road, a detour, that was not in our intended plan; they sometimes take us so far afield that we get lost and give up on ourselves.

A distraction can be cunning, can fool us into thinking and believing that it's not a distraction. We are brilliant and clever at this. Some of our distractions sound so logical, so intelligent that someone might say, "Why of course you'd do that instead of this." Or, "That makes good sense" or "Why not? What difference can it make?" And so we let ourselves off the hook, allow others to let us off the hook, and in turn do the same for them. No wonder we so often journey down a road of broken dreams barely tapping our potential.

Distractions are very close to my heart because I am a master at them.

As when I say, "I want to begin a painting." Here is what I often do. I choose the canvas, put it on my easel, even pick out the tubes of color— then lo and behold—I walk away! I create a distraction like turning on the TV, going to a movie, puttering around the house, phoning a family member I've been worried about, and on and on. Given that it does take some guts to approach a vacant canvas, there's that fear, that doubt. But when I wake up to what I really want to do, when I say, "I want to paint for creativity's sake" and "The hardest thing about creating is to begin," I usually begin. I turn on the music, dip my brush into the glorious color and move across the canvas to the music with a big smile on my face. (That was pretty benign but just you wait until we uncover some real monsters.) Hopefully, together, we can become more awake and aware and eliminate what we don't want, manifesting a deep satisfaction in our lives that we have not experienced before.

We do need to make distinctions about distractions. Not every pause, thought, action is a detour. Sometimes they enhance the dream, the vision, the commitment—we'll elaborate on this later on.

It all comes down to knowing who we are, being true to that, and doing what we really want to do.

Who We Are

Knowing who you are sounds like a big order. I choose to keep it simple—no need to delve into profound interpretation. Although this can be fun and interesting, even an ego booster, it can also create distractions!

How about "Who I am is a human being"? Then we might add, "Who I am is a human being who is writing a book." I like to minimize labels because they can separate us from one another and get us into judgments.

Since the only true time is the present, the only time that counts, then isn't who you are whatever you are being and/or doing now? Like, "Who I am is a human being experiencing a sunset" or "Who I am is a human being making love" or "Who I am is a human being creating a distraction." (Then identify the distraction!)

A great exercise is to stand outside of yourself, about three feet, and observe yourself whenever you are pulled to do so. No judgments, just be an observer, a witness to your thoughts, expressions, actions, etc. Then ask the question: "Who is the observer?"

(next)

Knowing who you are at any given moment will result in you being a person who is fully conscious and passionately engaged in life.

Doing What We Really Want to Do

"The truth shall set you free" is about knowing ourselves. So doing what we really want to do is an extension of knowing who we are. For example if I say, "Who I am is a human being who is a stand for being healthy" then what I really want to do is to have my actions support that. I will move from "I should exercise" to "I want to exercise" and find myself actually exercising with joy and freedom from guilt.

Saying "yes" when we really want to say "no" is a big one. When we can determine what and who supports our visions, our dreams, our lifestyles, etc. and what and who does not, we are awake! But just knowing is not always enough; it takes courage and love of self to be true to who we are and what we really want. When we become impeccably honest with ourselves, our journey becomes:

I took the road less traveled and that has made all the difference.

Robert Frost

Being authentic creates an opening for possibility.

Paradoxes

Webster defines a paradox as "a seemingly contradictory statement that expresses a possible truth."

Some examples:

1. In the dark of night I saw the light of day.

2. Surrender to win.

3. "Love is funny and it's sad

   Love is quiet or it's mad

   It's a good thing or it's bad

   —but beautiful!"

4. "I have a friend who has cancer and she's the healthiest person
   I know."

These are just a few examples and you can have fun adding to the list.

There will no doubt be contradictions/paradoxes in this book because our lives are full of them. This doesn't make wrong "a possible truth." We just don't tend to like paradoxes because they color a thing grey and we tend to like things a definite black or white. Then we don't have to figure anything out for ourselves. We don't have to stretch, to listen to what comes through us via our minds, our hearts, our souls. Trust who you are!

So I say, God bless our contradictions, the paradoxes. Let's bless anything that makes us taller—the long and the short of it.

Some paradoxes I have thought of . . .

distractions . . .

1. Comparing

I do not know when we began comparing ourselves to others. Perhaps when we made our grand entrance. Maybe it was our first day at school. I don't know but it's almost as automatic as breathing and certainly almost always unconscious. But making comparisons, more times than not, stops us in our tracks. This is a distraction that can be devastating to the creative process or to our motivation.

For instance, only recently I was in a phone conversation with someone close to me who is writing a children's book. She was raving about the Harry Potter books. I said, "Didn't that imagination inspire you?" She paused, "Well, not exactly! My story seems drab in comparison." Her voice had changed from joy to sadness as though she were giving up.

I can remember driving my beautiful girls and their classmates to school. The primping, the poking at themselves with "Oh! I wish I looked like Ann," or "Look at that! Look at that fat!"—all in their early teens. On the other hand a few years ago I asked my six-foot-tall daughter-in-law, "How did you handle your height when you were a teenager?" She laughed, "Oh I just knew that I was the biggest and the smartest!" Her healthy and wise choice gave her confidence. She was comfortable with herself!

Someone who all her life had carried the statement within herself, "I can't paint," met an artist/teacher who said to her, "You can paint because of what you see. Your eyes tell me that." She believed the artist/teacher, never again comparing herself to the works of art in galleries and museums and today she enjoys painting. Having let go of the comparing distraction that stopped her, she became free to discover her long suppressed creativity.

If we could have others inspire us, or we could simply appreciate them or learn from them, we'd be better off. The truth is that there is no one else on this earth like you. Literally! Try closing your eyes and visualizing six billion people holding hands and encircling the planet. Then visualize each person with different fingerprints, different DNA—each person unique, a whole and individual human being. Isn't that awesome?

I went to a huge bookstore before I started writing this and came away saying, "Who needs another book?" But then I remembered Brenda Uelands' words from *If You Want to Write.* She said, "Everybody is talented, original, and has something important to say." So I woke up, stopped creating the comparing distraction, and here I am writing! In reality, there's no one out there to compare yourself to because, again, in reality there's no one in this world like you—or like me.

Comparing Worksheet

How does this distraction keep you from being who <u>you are</u> and from doing

what you really want to do?

Literally stops me. Frustrates & depresses me.

xiety, *1. won't dress up & go "out" anymore, BC*
OMD, *a) I'm fat & everywill see. 'FATTER' than others*
epression *b) my hair + makeup - sweat. others aren't.*

fraid *2. work - multiple failures, poor reviews*
nervous *a) I'm no good, everyone is better.*
& start
again

What <u>actions</u> are you willing to take to be who <u>you are</u> and to do what you

really want to do? *Q: What "actions" are available? What*
ideas? HOW

2. Excuses

The first excuse that comes to mind is, "I don't have enough time." Sound familiar? We use it like a sacred and holy guarantee to get us in and/or out of almost anything.

And we totally believe one another when we say it and certainly convince ourselves. No questions asked. What a joke, although the joke's on us because we're unconscious of what we're believing. "I don't have enough time" is a myth. Most excuses are myths—distractions that keep us from taking responsibility for our lives. We make them up (creative beings that we are).

If the only real time is now, the only time that counts, that is ticking, then where is "enough time"? If now is the only time there is, isn't it then all the time there is?

It's been said that if you want to get something accomplished, go to a busy person. Why? You've got it—because they are usually completely present, conscious, and focused in the moment and committed to that moment. Also, an accomplishing busy person is usually organized. No clutter in the environment (seen or unseen).

Oh! I almost forgot. Do you know the road runner? He's habitually late and almost always in a hurry—complains about never catching up then makes himself even later by boring you with lengthy excuses. It's a wise saying: "Haste makes waste."

If we can live our lives not just one day at a time, but being and doing in the present time, plenty of time would appear as if with an elegant magic wand! (Once again, knowing who we are and what we really want to do are the priorities.)

Here is a second common excuse: "I don't feel like it." Good grief—how many times? We're not talking about being sick (although some believe we can go this far to avoid loving ourselves), but about creating an excuse not to do what we really want to do. For example, let's say you really want to exercise. You get all prepared, ready to go, and then, "Oh, I don't feel like it!" A feeling! So often the feeling wins, you give in and let it distract you. The time to exercise vanishes. But if we can wake up and say "I will not allow my feelings to tell me what to do" and then just do it, we're free! Do the thing to get the power.

And another: "I'm too old" or "I'm not old enough." We use our age as a limitation, an excuse, a myth. Much of it comes from the mind set out there that we buy and then own. "You're too old to do that—slow down!" or "You're too young to understand." All we've created to stunt our growth and creativity is almost criminal. The film and television industry insults us by deciding that we, the public, are only interested in viewing a certain age group. "I can't do that because I'm just a woman" is fortunately fading from sight because women took a stand to own their power. So too, this age myth will fade. There are many extraordinary examples of both elders and young-sters owning their power—they are gifts of inspiration to us. The turning tide will one day eliminate this excuse from our thinking.

"I'm tired!" I think it was Marianne Williamson who said, "We're not tired because we do too much but because we do too little." Often the doing in my head is so much that I literally can become exhausted and nau-seated worrying about how much I have to do. But then I pick up the first dirty dish, pay the first bill, make the commitment, write the first page—it's finished. The tiring work was in my head. ←

Or we might be doing a lot of what we don't want to do, like pleasing others or being resigned and settling for less. Being unconscious, "spinning our wheels"—working hard and getting nowhere while feeling resentment—certainly drains our energy. When I catch myself saying, "I'm tired" I ask, "What are you tired of?" I'll uncover whether or not I'm using it as an excuse or am truly out of physical energy and need to replenish it. I do know that when I'm madly in love with what I'm doing, my energy increases and joy is running the show.

"Not smart enough" gets us off the hook every time. "I don't have a degree" (or enough degrees). There are too many fine examples that expose this excuse as a myth. How about Einstein who flunked out and the famous writers, actors, artists, scientists, inventors, and billionaires who are too numerous to name? But they were unstoppable. They knew who they were and what they wanted to be, to do.

Just know, wise one, that your vision, your dream, your idea would not have come through you if you did not have the ability to manifest it. (Even if you're in a wheel chair.)

Excuses Worksheet

How does this distraction keep you from being who you are and from doing
what you really want to do? lifelong. I want to do (learn, etc)
"X" but "don't have time" "too old" "too fat"
"other priorities"

ALSO: Issue w/ self-care, sort of "unallowed" for
me to do recreation + relaxation. (guilt)
Bc been Mom focused on giving care to
others + not taking care of me.

So, I don't learn + do: glassblowing, yoga, zumba
fire spinning, spanish,

What actions are you willing to take to be who you are and to do what you
really want to do? What "actions" can be taken?
Simply catch myself making an excuse,
then examining it + deciding if I want
that, or not. Deeper urge/need?

Catching myself is 1/2 the battle.

3. Procrastinating

"Putting off 'til tomorrow what we can do today" follows on the heels of the excuse, "not enough time." But it needs to be listed as one of our distractions.

I was an old pro at this. Procrastination was a serious character flaw that ran my life. I had to confront it because it caused me such pain and harmed others. I was oblivious to keeping my word and following things through to completion. I was so paralyzed in putting off everything, that beginning what I really wanted to do had no entry! I was convinced that putting off something actually made it easier. Like Scarlet: "I'll think about it tomorrow." Believe it or not, I would sometimes toss the monthly bills praying that they would go away, and then came the phone calls from collectors. True, this was after a divorce and I knew nothing about money, etc. But procrastinating was the culprit and I discovered that "tomorrow never comes," as I just buried myself deeper and deeper.

Awareness is the first step. Take some time to examine the reasons you are procrastinating. For me it was a fear of succeeding, not of failing, along with a fear of responsibility. Waking up to being responsible and loving myself enough to have my well being be a priority finally had me living in the now. When you pretty much eliminate procrastinating you pretty much eliminate much of the stress in your life. A freedom and satisfaction comes in that is downright delightful. Isn't it a thrill to cross those things off your list? Or to say, "I did it!" There's no other feeling quite like it: being victorious!

Procrastinating Worksheet

How does this distraction keep you from being who you are and from doing what you really want to do? *Things dont get done. EX: Too big of project. Don't know where to start, or how to do it, or it is very time consuming, and/or I still need to buy supplies or do research etc. So, I do something else. I might do the research 1st, then nothing further. Often "overwhelm" is the reason I don't start. EX: fire costume & ABC 'construction' costume disaster.*

What actions are you willing to take to be who you are and to do what you really want to do? *Same Q: what "actions"?*

4. Complaining (and Blaming)

Webster's synonyms for complain: "to grumble, to beef, to gripe, to squawk, to croak, to bellyache." No wonder it's a challenge to be subjected to it. Although the complainer seeks sympathy we often want to respond with "blah, blah, blah." Complaining and blaming are, more often than not, connected. It's hard to find one without the other. And it's usually about being blind to our own responsibility in the matter. It's not what happens but how we handle what happens. Have you ever observed yourself complaining to someone who is no longer there, to a "blank wall"? Our complaints don't move the stars, and they certainly do not move others!

Complaining, and blaming someone or something, is such a powerless place to be. But we think it's the perfect solution that gets us off the hook; it never works because the same stuff *(our stuff)* keeps reappearing. Complaining and blaming keep us from looking at ourselves. Here's a typical complaint (that therapists milk dry): "I can't help it! I'm this way because of my parents, etc., etc." Or it could be a host of various becauses. Whatever we're in denial about or refuse to confront keeps us enslaved as if we're set in cement, unmovable. Certainly this is a self-created distraction that keeps us from being who we are and doing what we really want to do. Realize that there is no one or no-thing working against you.

Giving our power away to the ordinary weather conditions is a common one. Or there's the person in a restaurant who complains constantly and is totally insensitive to the waiter's listening. Jason, my 16 year old grandson, said, "Complaining is never constructive. An airline passenger complaining about his seat might feel better afterwards but the stewardess doesn't feel better."

And my friend Marie (who is being a super woman in a difficult marriage) said, "My complaining and blaming always fell on deaf ears and went nowhere—a waste of my time and energy. And afterwards I always felt exhausted and terrible. Complaining and blaming is a real killer of self-esteem." Her marriage is better.

There's always a kinder, a gentler way. Complaining and blaming never get us there. (This distraction spills over into another distraction, "judging," that will be discussed later.)

 Acceptance, flexibility, appreciation, gratitude, and last but not least, a sensitivity to the other's listening will give us a start in a new direction. Let's remember to look in our direction not another's. An astrologer friend of mine teaches, "There's no one out there!"

Complaining Worksheet

Blaming [handwritten above title]

How does this distraction keep you from being who you are and from doing what you really want to do? *Kind of Excuse. But/And also "Explanation" of why the deck looks like shit (I hired Hawaii & he did an awful job) or why the ABC party / petting zoo wasnt fun (BC the people I knew werent there)*

Complaing pushes people away (AML.) Makes Boss etc think I'm negative and Poor employee.

What actions are you willing to take to be who you are and to do what you really want to do?

5. Addictions/Habits

Even Webster overlaps the distinctions between addictions and habits. I think of a habit as being an action that is repetitive over a period of time and is usually spontaneous and seemingly without thought. It lives and thrives in unawareness and can be constructive, destructive or neutral. The progression is habit to addiction, not the other way around, and every habit does not lead to an addiction. An addiction is usually self-defeating and destructive. It is the mother of distractions that creates every other distraction that exists, an all consuming monster that eats away at our holy reason for being.

Medical authorities in chemical dependency say addiction is, "continued compulsive use despite adverse consequences." And I believe that is true for the addictions to gambling (or money), belief systems, shopping, relationships, computers, sex, food, seminars ("seminar junkies"), possessions, control issues, TV, sports, and on and on.

Here's a terrific definition of insanity that seems appropriate here: "Making the same destructive choices and expecting different results."

Dr. Lee Jampolsky says in his book, *Healing the Addictive Mind,* "We can't hide in our addiction and experience love at the same time." Addiction seems to create hiding, dishonesty, secrecy. And certainly without question it keeps us from being who we are and doing what we really want to do.

I know something about addiction. You see, I am a recovered drug addict of thirty-seven years. Alcohol was my drug of choice. I say the controversial "recovered" instead of recovering because that addiction does not run my life anymore. That addiction is no longer an issue, not a subject matter, not in my sensory memory. And it wouldn't occur to me to have a drink any more than it would enter my mind to have a cigarette (nicotine and I parted company about thirty years ago). Besides, we can't go back!

I believe in healing. Another book could be written about that period in my life and about the devastation of addiction. Suffice it to say that the hardest work I've ever done or ever will do was during the time of my alcohol addiction. I was in the restraints of a mental and emotional obsession combined with an overpowering physical craving that rendered me helpless. I couldn't win! But when I became ready to call forth all of the willingness available, the chains of helplessness were broken and I could see light at the end of my tunnel of darkness.

Probably my most far-reaching and effective 12th step work came from a vision to create Alcoholics Anonymous in the Soviet Union in the early 1980s. Enough brave souls took on this vision with a project that we called, "Creating a Sober World." Our first trip in April 1986 resulted in the first open A.A. meetings for the Soviet alcoholic. Today A.A. and Alanon thrive in Russia and its adjacent countries. This is another story about commitment, possibility and being who we are.

Have the courage, the willingness to identify your destructive habits and addictions on the following worksheets. Then get help, do the work, and discover being open, being free. Glorious!

I would like to end this distraction by elaborating on a statement from the poet, Rilke: "Live the question now." When we can become patient and trusting enough to just be in the question then eventually we will experience ourselves being in the answer.

Addictions/Habits Worksheet

How does this distraction keep you from being who you are and from doing what you really want to do?

What actions are you willing to take to be who you are and to do what you really want to do?

6. Bigotries

Webster's definition of bigotry: "Obstinate and unreasoning attachment to one's own beliefs and opinions with intolerance of beliefs and opinions opposed to them. Behavior ensuing from such a condition."

Surprised? "Bigot" is an ugly word that we do not want to be associated with. "I'm not a bigot," you say! or "I don't have any bigotries!" Well dear friend, look again!

When I was creating the "Beyond Bigotry" workshop I knew that I had to look deeply within to uncover my own bigotries if the workshop was to have integrity and heart. I was devastated and in shock! Two bigotries arose from their graves: the homeless and enormously heavy people. Walking in a city, if a homeless person appeared I would cross the street to avoid any confrontation or connection. The same response would occur when a heavy person appeared—avoidance at any cost. I made them invisible! (But only after I had judged them thoroughly.) Our thoughts are powerful and go out there. Like the wind, we see the results but not the wind itself. I always feared that "those others" felt my bigotry, my judgment. But what it did to me was far worse. I would feel ashamed, depressed, unloved, and full of guilt.

We can pretend, cover it up, but bigotry makes slaves of us, steals our time, our energy, and stunts our growth. It is definitely a distraction that keeps us from being who we are and doing what we really want to do.

I chose to heal my bigotries by literally facing them. I began connecting and communicating at every opportunity. The results were astounding. There is never a conversation with a homeless person that doesn't leave both of us smiling and radiating joy. Lately I've become really brave by asking *them* for money. (Who I am is ending hunger in the world.) They love it and often contribute. I believe that each and every one of us *wants* to contribute.

And I am always amazed with enormous people. Recently a large woman was my seat companion on a plane. She was indeed large in every way, a Ph.D. who was devoted to youth at risk. Her heart filled the sky we were flying through.

No one is born a bigot, just like God did not create the boundaries. It's our responsibility to identify our bigotries and discover where they come from. Look at your labels and your attachment to them. When you can see bigotry as a distraction in your life you will want to move beyond it.

I Am Not I

I am not I.
I am this one
Walking beside me whom I do not see,
Whom at times I manage to visit,
And at other times I forget.
The one who remains silent when I talk,
The one who forgives, sweet, when I hate,
The one who takes a walk when I am indoors,
The one who will remain standing when I die.

Juan Ramon Jimenez

Bigotry Worksheet

How does this distraction keep you from being who you are and from doing what you really want to do?

What actions are you willing to take to be who you are and to do what you really want to do?

7. Minding Their Business

This distraction is a major troublemaker for most of us, especially for parents and spouses. But neighbors, friends, co-workers, those who serve us—even sports, television and film celebrities (including the characters they play) and our politicians steal our precious time. Why is it so much easier to mind someone else's business than to mind one's own? Is it easier to put our minds on them with our judgments, assumptions, opinions and answers? And let's not forget the fantasies!

Isn't it incredible how we would prefer knowing what's best for someone else rather than figuring out what's best for ourselves?

As a single parent of six children, cutting off the parenting when it was appropriate was difficult. I'm such a Mom! It had taken all of me for many years. I was dependent on *being* a Mom. Letting go of Barry, Christopher, David, Deborah, Hope and Linda took major work. (And then there was reinventing Faith!) Today when I disagree with their choices I make every effort to remember that they are adults on their own journeys to learn what they are given to learn, and that they are my gifts—blessings that make my life rich and full. They are my teachers, my partners, and my gorgeous children.

Gossip has been defined as character assassination. Here again is a destructive, unconscious activity that is minding another's business instead of our own. I believe that we love it because it fills an emptiness and gets us off the hook. Saying, "the poor thing" seems to make us feel richer, better than. It's so much easier and more fun to point out another's wrong doing rather than face our own. But all of it backfires, doesn't it?

When we are being nosy neighbors, worrying, dictating, directing, controlling others' lives—or gossiping, we are not focused on who *we* are and/or what *we* are doing. Or when we are addicted to soap operas, celebrity lives, politicians, sports figures, crime figures, etc., we are saying that we value their lives more than we value our own.

There is a huge distinction between "minding their business" and loving others. Loving others is in direct proportion to loving yourself. Love of Self (not an ego oriented me, me, me!) will have us *being* who we are and *doing* what we really want to do.

Minding Their Business Worksheet

How does this distraction keep you from being who you are and from doing what you really want to do?

What actions are you willing to take to be who you are and to do what you really want to do?

Time Out

Being fully awake and conscious does not require us to be in constant motion. So let's take time out, breathe deeply, and relax into some laughter. I'm reminded of one of the few jokes that I remember:

> Two ants were on top of a cereal box. One ant was running around and around in a circle. The other ant said, "Why are you running around in a circle?" The running ant panted, "Can't you read the directions? It says, 'Tear around the dotted line!'"

I've often thought that a visiting alien, seeing us racing around to and fro might conclude: a species gone mad.

Take time out to become balanced. Being nothing, doing nothing, just letting "I am" be enough for a while—go deeply within: listen, feel, love. Allow time to daydream, to do tai-chi or yoga, go for a slow walk. Silence. Peace.

It's been said that meditation is love. When we can be in a pure state of love and gratitude we become one with all that is. Extraordinary visions and ideas come out of this seeming nothingness. Haven't you said, "Where did that come from?"

Fully aware human beings are balanced, whole. They seem to be able to do it all with an ease, a grace, a presence, a focus, and a comfortable poise that lights up the world. They know who they are and are doing what they really want to do. And they are never "tearing around the dotted line." We have the same possibilities! No kidding!

So let's take time out to laugh at ourselves—to be still and to know! We will then be ready and eager to slay the next dragon.

I think continually of those
        who were truly great,
The names of those who
        in their lives
        fought for life,
Who wore at their hearts
        the fire's center
Born of the sun they
        traveled toward the sun.
And left the vivid air
        signed with their honor.

Stephen Spender

8. Boredom

When you say, "I'm bored" you're saying, "I'm stuck," "I'm tired," "I don't care," "I'm bored with me," "I'm bored with my life," "I'm not interested in anything."

Boredom comes from within. It is soil, fertile with the elements that attract mischief, trouble, craziness. To ease the pain and make it go away we can reach for something or someone outside of ourselves—like food, alcohol or drugs, shopping, travel, or a lover. Boredom is the birthing place for self-destructive choices that lead to addictions and heartaches. It is certainly a distraction that keeps us from being who we are and doing what we really want to do.

I say that boredom is a sin. And I define sin as anything that separates us from our Source. It is a close cousin to depression and completely self-involved. It's not easy to awaken from a state of being that seems to hold you powerless. It takes an enormous amount of willing and screaming, "I've had enough!" Open your eyes and see that you're more attracted to dying than to living.

And none of us *want* to be boring people. But trust me—when you are bored, you *are* boring!

Leo was driving me to the Reno airport in his company's van. I asked him, "Leo are you ever bored?" "A lot," he said. I then asked him, "Where do you think that comes from?" "Oh, that's a good question!" He drove silently for a few miles down the mountain. Then he said, "It comes from my life!" I complimented him and said, "Leo, what do you really want to do?" "I want to be a concrete truck driver but I have to study to get a license." I suggested, "Are you bored when you're studying?" He laughed, "No, I'm not!" I encouraged him to go for it, saying he deserved to be who he wanted to be and to do what he really wanted to do. His energy shifted and he thanked me when we said good-bye.

Some opposites of boredom are humor, commitment, gratitude, love, appreciation of ourselves and others, action, creating, learning, listening, hearing, seeing, helping others less fortunate than ourselves, being engaged in something—passion, joy.

I guess nothing gets our attention like a near death experience, a wake-up call that has us being grateful for being alive. But *you* can get your attention! Your life is precious, is worth every lovely moment that you live into it. What a glorious gift to treasure for the short amount of time that it is given to us. Make it count!

Boredom Worksheet

How does this distraction keep you from being who you are and from doing what you really want to do?

What actions are you willing to take to be who you are and to do what you really want to do?

9. Apathy

Apathy and boredom are twins. It is difficult to discern which one comes first. I see them as creating one another. Both distractions come from complete self-involvement—selfishness if you will.

Apathy holds all of humanities' problems in place: bigotry, violence, greed, hunger, and the destruction of our Earth home, to identify a few.

Apathetic human beings are uncaring, passionless, unconcerned, and uninterested in anything or anyone outside of their small worlds. They not only do not respond to humanities' needs but they do not even see them: no awareness or sensitivity. Change, much less giving of themselves, simply terrifies them. If only they knew that giving is receiving, that giving one's money, time, love, energy, creativity, etc. results in receiving more of the same for one's self.

I doubt if many apathetic people will be attracted to reading this book. Just know that apathy needs to be confronted with compassion and understanding. Love is the healer when you are conscious of apathy within yourself or within someone else. Healing is the possibility.

Ending this chapter on a lighter note, I'm reminded of a remark by my daughter, Linda: "I can tell you why we haven't been visited by any aliens—we're still killing each other!"

Enough said.

> This is the true joy in life:
> ...being used for a purpose recognized
> by yourself as a mighty one;
> ...being a force of nature
> instead of a feverish, selfish little
> clod of ailments and grievances
> complaining that the world will not
> devote itself to making you happy.
>
> I am of the opinion that my life
> belongs to the whole community,
> and as long as I live, it is my privilege
> to do for it whatever I can.
>
> *George Bernard Shaw*

Apathy Worksheet

How does this distraction keep you from being who you are and from doing what you really want to do?

What actions are you willing to take to be who you are and to do what you really want to do?

10. Insecurities/Fears

E.N. Griswold says, "Security is seeking after the illusion of certainty." Shakespeare says, "Security is mortals' chiefest enemy." We want guarantees, we crave certainties, freedom from danger, safety, always having what we think is enough. I could write hundreds of pages on this subject. (This thought almost stopped me from writing it at all.)

We will be in a freer and more comfortable place if we can accept the non-existence of security as something out there: security is not a thing but a state of being. We must recognize that change is the only constant, the only certainty. Knowing this helps us to greet change as expected rather than as a surprise, and then perhaps to drop the resistance to changing ourselves.

The insecurities and fears that we allow to stop us are numberless. We are afraid we will fail, afraid we will succeed, afraid it won't be perfect, afraid of what others will think or say, and on and on.

I can only give you my experience. Like everyone else, I feel that panic, that crippling fear, just before I go on the stage or to the podium. What happens? I feel the fear and acknowledge it, but it's too late to leave, to run. So

I walk to the podium and begin to speak. Often I've said, "I'm nervous." Or, "I'm really terrified being up here." The fear disappears. An actor walks on the stage and becomes his character. The fear disappears. Before I paint or write the fears often paralyze me. But beginning the painting, beginning the writing, eliminates the fears. Why? What is it that makes fear disappear?

When we have developed a true love of ourselves and of others we will not be so concerned about others' opinions. An opinion is something that anyone is free to have; it's not necessarily a truth for you or about you. Remembering that there is not one really secure human being on Earth should stop us once and for all from being afraid of one another. What a joke!

George Bernard Shaw said, "Our plan gives no guarantee that we shall get the steam engine." Maybe, but maybe not—it could be something even better.

A talented Vietnamese friend said, "Security is Love!" Thank you, Kim. So simple yet huge.

Also I've noticed that there is no insecurity or fear in the present moment. They are always in the past or in the future, mostly in the future!

Finally, let's try to remember that being afraid of not having enough when in truth we have *more* than enough creates a hunger that is never satisfied.

I lived on the shady side of the road and watched my
    neighbors' gardens across the way reveling in the
    sunshine.

I felt I was poor, and from door to door went with my
    hunger.

The more they gave me from their careless abundance
    the more I became aware of my beggar's bowl.

Till one morning I awoke from my sleep at the sudden
    opening of my door, and you came and asked for
    alms.

In despair I broke the lid of my chest open and was
    startled into finding my own wealth.

Rabindranath Tagore

Insecurities/Fears Worksheet

How does this distraction keep you from being who you are and from doing what you really want to do?

What actions are you willing to take to be who you are and to do what you really want to do?

11. Beliefs/Opinions

Our lives are controlled by our beliefs and opinions. We create them or choose them to survive our fears and insecurities, sometimes just to survive. We're always in hope that they will improve us, improve our lives. But so often they put us in a box—box us in. We become addicted, dependent on our beliefs, on being right, and glued to our positions like figures in stone: unmovable. The labels that come out of our beliefs are worn with pride and arrogance, separating us from one another.

Our insecurities can go so deep that believing someone else, listening to someone else, following someone else, becomes our priority. We give away our power, our identity, to someone or something else, so nonchalantly, so carelessly, often unconsciously. We cannot seem to trust the authority within ourselves—to listen to it, to believe it, to create and choose from it. Of course it's much easier (we mistakenly think) to just have someone else or something else tell us what or what not to do, to run our lives! It's easier not to take responsibility, easier not to think outside of our comfortable boxes, easier to blame something else or someone else if it doesn't work out—

easier not to think for ourselves. What a monstrous price to pay for the crucifixion of our creativity, our awesome uniqueness, our special expression of love and intelligence!

Of course we have our beliefs and opinions. I just want us to be awake and conscious! Do my beliefs and opinions include or exclude, separate or unite? Do they have me being more, feeling more, trusting more, growing more, listening and following my authority more? Am I more because of my beliefs and opinions? Am I willing to risk, to go for it, to manifest my visions, to really be in the world, to be free?

Seeing a teacher in every one and every experience keeps me teachable and open. You, the reader, teach me to remember honesty as I write this book even as it hopefully will teach you something as you read it. Let's always be inquiring and trust ourselves to uncover the distractions that keep us from being who we are and doing what we really want to do.

As children we needed our parents and other adults to train us and guide us for our survival and growth. To paraphrase: "But when I became a grownup I put away childish things." To me this means knowing that I am enough, that I have been given everything and everyone I need, that nothing is missing!

Beliefs and Opinions Worksheet

How does this distraction keep you from being who you are and from doing what you really want to do?

What actions are you willing to take to be who you are and to do what you really want to do?

12. Disorder

When there is disorder in our lives we are distracted—big time.

Disorder and order look like:

Disorder	Order
Confusion	Understanding
Chaos	Harmony
Unfinished business	Finished business
Imbalance	Balance
Insanity	Sanity
Dysfunctional	Functional
Out of place	In place
Unclear	Clear
Broken	Repaired
Separation	Unity
Lost	Found
Dirty	Clean
Hate/Violence	Love/Forgiveness

War	Peace
Incomplete	Complete
Prejudice/bigotry	Acceptance
Disagreement	Agreement
Resentment/Anger	Forgiveness/Love
Inefficient	Efficient
Inappropriate	Appropriate
Hidden/Closed	Revealed/Open
Loud/Noise	Quiet/Silence
Unhealthy	Healthy
Illness	Wellness
Stress	Calm
Cluttered	Uncluttered
Worry/Fear	Trust/Faith
Drunk	Sober
Unorganized	Organized
Agitated	Relaxed
Hunger/Craving	Fulfillment/Satisfaction

Denial	Awareness
Running late	On time
Forgetting	Remembering
Unconscious	Conscious

Did I say, "big time"? You will be identifying many *more* disorders that create distractions in your life.

Have fun!

For many years I have said, "as within so without." These words help me to be aware, to see what is really going on with me and how that is being reflected in my relationships, my environment, my thinking, feeling, speaking, and actions—all of it! It's a perfect barometer that tells it exactly the way it is.

It's sort of like: what I swallow into my body (even when no one is watching) will eventually show up and be seen by all as a healthy or unhealthy physical being. "As within so without!" Or, what I swallow mentally, emotionally, or spiritually will have me being worse off or better off.

My youngest daughter, Deborah, organizes people's lives. She calls her business "First Things First." As a labor of love she offered to assist me with several drawers full of photographs. (Did I mention a hidden disorder?) No one else knew what a total chaotic mess lurked inside those drawers. But each day for years they reminded me and I found myself saying, "I should handle those damn photographs!" At least I was conscious enough to remember them.

It took us two days, filling up the tossed ones in three huge trash bags. Separate piles were mailed to family members and a big photo journal was created for me. At a later time Deborah helped me organize my writings. I can't begin to describe the freedom from those distractions. Thank you, Debs!

The person in my life who has inspired me the most in the art of letting go and being orderly is my middle daughter, Hope Adele. She is a Master! Throwing out and cleaning out closets, drawers, etc. gives her real joy and satisfaction. Thank you, Hope Adele!

And in relationships: when something needs to be communicated (like an apology, a thank you, a truth) the relationship is uncomfortable and we are ill at ease until we provide what's missing. This moves us from incomplete to complete.

Today is Saturday. I began this chapter this morning and I can't help but laugh. I had cleaning help this morning to clean behind my washer and dryer—Maytags that never need fixing or replacing. I fully expected creepy crawlers to appear in all their glory. Termite inspectors and gardeners are also scheduled to come today. There are no accidents dear friends!

Just getting a few disorders eliminated makes you feel so great, *and* so smart. I've lived in chaotic disorder and I've lived in divine order. I'll take the latter any time.

Disorder Worksheet

How does this distraction keep you from being who you are and from doing what you really want to do?

What actions are you willing to take to be who you are and to do what you really want to do?

13. Traditions

Webster defines traditions as "beliefs rooted in the experience of the past and exerting an influence on the present. Inherited reputation or memory."

I think of them as customs, ideas and creations that are handed down, coming from the past. They never come from the present moment: fresh, new, different, and original! We live in traditions most of the time. The list is lengthy but here are a few examples: holidays, countries, religions, manners, styles, rules and laws, governments, art, education, family, etc., etc., etc.

Traditions give us a sense of permanence, security, safety, predictability, and comfort. Unchangeable, they are sure things we can count on.

But traditions can also keep us from being who we are and doing what we really want to do. They can keep us rigidly stuck and unable to move in a different direction toward a better solution, a more rewarding result—opening more to more. They can create a stagnation that kills passion and produces inertia and apathy within ourselves and within humanity as a whole.

Some family traditions are crippling as when a son or a daughter is bound by tradition in his or her choice of career. Remember *Fiddler on the Roof?* It is the story of a Jewish father who has to confront the untraditional choices of his daughters, and on another level, the story of the sons and daughters who dare to be themselves—who have the courage to know, "I am not my father" or "I am not my mother."

On a lighter note, I can remember one Christmas when my oldest son, Barry, came home from college. I thought it would be fun to have a white tree for a change. Barry became so upset that he couldn't eat his favorite meal that I had prepared. The traditional green tree won out after a family vote. It took another year or two before a white tree was accepted. Today we all have fake trees to help the environment!

We are indeed creatures of habit. Let's be conscious enough to see the dull patterns, to ask the brave questions, and to have a willingness to create, to open, to fly.

Traditions Worksheet

How does this distraction keep you from being who you are and from doing what you really want to do?

What actions are you willing to take to be who you are and to do what you really want to do?

14. Toxic Influence

Most of us are well aware of the word "toxic." We inhale, consume, and hear toxins. But I want to alert us to some other forms of toxic influences that we'd be better off without.

A big one that comes to mind is toxic people in our lives. Those who exploit us, exhaust us, make us nuts and ready to doubt ourselves, selfish souls who seem to be incapable of offering us support and a healthy give and take.

Recognizing those who are given to jealousy, bullying and all of the above was once impossible for me. It just never occurred to me that anyone would be jealous or envious or manipulative. A willingness to practice the Alanon program brought me out into the sunlight. Putting my own well-being as a priority was a first for me—a new freedom that I cherish today. Loving myself enough, I now attract loving. And if it's not forthcoming I simply let it go and get on with my life. I don't spend a lot of time anymore recovering from someone.

Another toxic influence is exposing ourselves to darkness: watching too many depressing television news shows, going to negative movies, listening to gloomy complaining or heavy music and/or reading too much blood and gore. This darkness creates upsetting dreams and thoughts, causes depression and drained energy. It pulls us in like a magnet. But a sunrise or sunset fills us with beauty and inspiration and creative energy.

Lastly, imbalance! Being out of balance can also have a toxic influence on our perceptions and desires, on what we express and manifest. I used to feel out of balance without a man. Really, I felt that I was tilted, on a slant. Everything was missing! But after many disastrous choices I was forced to confront my imbalance. It took a whale of a lot of work to finally experience my wholeness and completeness—to enjoy my own company, to appreciate being alone but not lonely. I am never lonely! It's a bloomin' miracle! Nothing is missing and it's a thrill to be alive to love. I adore men, but no more live-ins, thank you very much.

It's also important to balance our feminine and masculine. My oldest daughter Linda suggests that women should ride horses, play sports to bring out their masculine and men should be in and around water to bring out their feminine because water—especially the ocean—represents the mother earth. It also means non-resistance, fluidity and flow. Possibilities abound!

Have fun listing the toxic influences that cause you to forget who you are and what you really want to do.

Toxic Influences Worksheet

How does this distraction keep you from being who you are and from doing what you really want to do?

What actions are you willing to take to be who you are and to do what you really want to do?

15. Irresponsibility

I think of responsibility as response-ability, the ability to respond. When we fail at this all else fails. Ignorance, not hearing, not seeing, being deaf, blind and dumb if you will, still does not let us off the hook. I am reminded of a great line in the film, "Wyatt Earp," when Doc Holliday says to Wyatt, "There is no hook my friend, there's only what you do!" It is the ability and willingness to see what is missing, what is needed and then to be responsible for producing it. What a difference this would make in our lives and in the world.

Jumping to conclusions, making assumptions, forgetting that it's all in the set-up can cause disastrous results: the overtime, the drained energy, the chaos we could eliminate if we became responsible enough to confront it, to check it out, to set it up ahead of the appointed time.

For example, when I visit someone or someone visits me I make every effort to communicate his or her needs and expectations and my needs and expectations. Taking responsibility in our relationships and their related events leads to experiences pretty free of surprises, misunderstandings and disappointments. This leaves more quality time for relating instead of "Oh, I thought you'd like it that way," etc., etc.

Responsible speaking (being sensitive to the other's listening) and responsible listening (really hearing not only what's said but what isn't without making assumptions) create satisfying results.

Then there's our first priority, being responsible for ourselves. Haven't you noticed that when you make your own well-being the number one priority all confusion falls away? I love being with those who know who they are and are doing what they really want to do. There's a clarity, a serenity, a loving energy that spills over—like a cleansing, a healing. They also instinctively know the distinction between responsibilities. Recognizing when it's appropriate to take responsibility in any given situation and when it is not has been a tough lesson for me. The two teachers who help me the most are the Hunger Project and Alanon. As I stated earlier, "Who I am is a stand to end hunger and poverty in the world." This is also the mission of the Hunger Project. But we do not feed people or give them handouts. We give them the opportunity to end their own poverty by empowering them (through training, workshops, etc.). Every human being hungers to know who he/she is. I recall the trip to Africa with the Hunger Project and my youngest daughter, Deborah. We were visiting the poverty stricken villages via bus. Debs and I had goody bags filled with things like toothbrushes, snacks, cosmetics, etc. But after being with the first village we hid the bags under our seats. What we encountered were clean, beautiful, colorfully dressed, dignified, joyful human beings. *And* they were in an uneducated state of poverty. It was so evident that giving them tokens or crumbs from our abundance would be demeaning and irresponsible. We got it! We saw first-hand the extraordinary principles of the Hunger Project and the magnificence of human beings. I am moved again by remembering this experience.

Alanon has helped me to say "no" to my children and others. If honoring their requests would keep them irresponsible and dependent, I say "no." If on the other hand, it would offer them a possibility, an opportunity to become more responsible, independent, and productive—I might say "yes." It's a tricky one and I've made more mistakes than I care to mention.

Being responsible for my own well-being is still a blind spot sometimes. As I write this, I'm on Maui in Kapalua, visiting my oldest grandson, Cooper. My middle daughter, Hope Adele, and her two teenagers live in Makawao.

Yesterday I had a few hours alone being with the beautiful water, the palms, and the soft air. I almost spoiled it by wishing that they could be with me to share it. But I shot up and said, "You deserve this time, this experience. Relish it!" And I did. Today I look forward to being with them, sharing this special place.

I believe that each of us has the ability to respond. If it's missing we need to be aware that it's missing. Therapy may be needed. But if we desire to be more, to love more, to live more, we can "call it forth, pull it in" and take response-ability to a new level.

All That Is

Call it forth, pull it
in, —
Light your fire with Love,
sweet Love,
Awakening you to seeing
All that lives, all that
moves
And has its Being
All for you!

Faith Fayman Strong 7/01

Irresponsibility Worksheet

How does this distraction keep you from being who you are and from doing what you really want to do?

What actions are you willing to take to be who you are and to do what you really want to do?

16. Being Immovable

It's comforting to know that we're not alone. Every human being has been in this place, so don't despair! We just want to recognize it, to identify it, to confront it, heal it, and move on. Move! Move! Move!

Immovable resembles being right—so positional that you become paralyzed, so unwilling to bend, to change, that your life looks like it's been set on "hold." This is a huge distraction that keeps us from being who we are and doing what we really want to do. The creative process cannot be born in this place. When we create we move! Moving is growing—looking in a new direction, opening to another way, another thought, a deeper feeling, opening to see more, hear more, be more!

Being immovable is being resigned, taking all for granted, being overwhelmed. Sometimes moving means *getting* quiet, *being* still. Sometimes moving might mean doing what we think we don't want to do in order to delay gratification, to move out of resignation, comfort, old patterns and pretending. Begin by saying, "I'm the guy who can do it" instead of the usual, "Let the other guy do it!" Sometimes we will end up discovering that we *are* doing what we really want to do after all. A stunning and clear paradox! As I said before, if an idea comes to you, chances are you're the one who's been chosen to manifest it. Don't let it be lost—you're the one!

One thing that gets me going is wanting to leave behind a life that was full of creativity, contribution, love, responsibility, and satisfaction—just in case this is the only life I have. So whatever moves you, use it and move it!

Immovable might look like this little poem of mine:

Immovable

I don't look like a rock—
But I feel heavy and loaded
with dirt,
Buried deep in my self,
unwilling to move.
An unchanging position,
going unnoticed
In this predictable state
of motionless ease.
Waiting to live, frightened
of you—
Afraid to be me.

Faith Fayman Strong 8/01

Being Immovable Worksheet

How does this distraction keep you from being who you are and from doing what you really want to do?

What actions are you willing to take to be who you are and to do what you really want to do?

17. Expectations/Hope

There is only a slight distinction between expectation and hope. Webster defines expectation as "the act of waiting, looking forward...assumption." And hope is defined as the act of "cherishing a desire with expectation." I regard both expectations and hope as distractions that keep us from being who we are and doing what we really want to do.

When we're waiting and/or looking forward for something to happen or for someone to do something, we're not being, we're not doing; we're in a no-thing place that produces nothing. Expecting and hoping keep us powerless and useless, whereas believing and knowing create commitment, action and the manifestation. There's no expectation or hope in the present moment. When we are consciously living, being responsible and loving ourselves and others in the present moment, expectation and hope have no entrance.

The weddings, honeymoons, New Year's eves, elections, relationships (parents and children, friendships, husbands and wives, lovers, employers and employees) that crumble as the result of impossible hopes and expectations could fill the spaces of the universe.

As a parent, letting go of hope and expectations is probably the toughest assignment that I've been given to handle. I think I've received a pretty high grade because not one of my six children has followed in my footsteps. It always makes me smile when one of them says, "I want your approval, Mom." I respond with, "No you don't or you wouldn't be choosing what you're choosing."

Years ago I read, "Good parents raise their children to leave them." To have our children approve of *their own* choices is what counts, not *our* hopes for them.

I really believe that we use wanting others' approval and "living up to their expectations" as an excuse, a distraction not to take our responsibility in the matter—especially when timid souls become followers, never realizing their greatness, their own personal journey. When that happens it's a tragedy, a loss for all of us.

When I don't have hope or expectations I don't have disappointment, blame, guilt, hurt, anger, grief, and sadness. But a surprise always catches me off guard (no control, right?)—anything unexpected, not hoped for or even imagined.

Like the electricity going out! What works, when we can remember it, is being creative. Have fun with it, and keep it all in perspective.

A sudden death, accident, etc. is another matter; this kind of distraction needs our presence, time, and energy. This is life showing up, testing our strength, love, courage, character, and compassion, and in the final scene making us better human beings.

Knowing that each of us is on a personal, unique journey, making our own choices from that uniqueness, helps to steer us clear of expectations and hope. Believing, *deeply* believing that all is working for our ultimate good brings us peace of mind and a lighter step.

Expectations/Hope Worksheet

How does this distraction keep you from being who you are and from doing what you really want to do?

What actions are you willing to take to be who you are and to do what you really want to do?

18. Low Self Worth

The last distraction for this book is the great grandaddy of all distractions. Every other distraction (including others you will think of) sit on top of this one. Low self worth is the foundation, the "bottom line" for all of it.

Sometimes it is obvious but so often it is disguised. For example, the one in rags and dirt who has obviously lost *his* memory, forgetting *his* magnificence as a human being. Or the seeming successful one, all puffed up with *his* success, but who within is insecure and terrified of losing it. This fear of losing what we have comes from guilt, feeling unworthy, and a very deep lack of confidence. I have been privileged to know a few celebrities in the TV and film industry. And as gorgeous as they are, as talented and gifted and sensitive, the fear of losing it is always there—always underneath the surface. That's why they, like *all* of us, soak up and adore praise and appreciation.

I'm not wise enough (See? There it goes!) to know exactly where this tendency comes from in each of us. There are some very old sayings like "You are born in sin" or "We are lowly worms" or "You are nothing" or "You are powerless" etc., etc., that have been with us since the beginning of time. But what about the sayings in *your* time, in *my* time: awful things that were said to us when we were children and up to the present? Of course, I can remember tons of remarks that left their scars, but one example stands out. I was sitting at my desk in a sixth grade classroom. I was having trouble with a math question. The teacher came to my desk and instead of helping me, loudly said, "Faith, you're beautiful but dumb." I ran out of the classroom and didn't return to school for two days. I decided that not only was I dumb but that I would never understand math. These became facts that ran my life! Later, while in therapy, I discovered that the teacher was physically very unattractive and was coming from her own insecurities and envies. It is amazing to me how we pounce on the negative stuff as being the truth about us.

Low self worth is fertile soil for sowing dangerous beliefs and ideas. Evil leaders whose motives stem from greed and lust for power could not exist without those of low self worth who choose to follow them without question. This is the extreme example of not taking responsibility for one's life—an "easier, softer way"! But is it really? What gives us the greatest satisfaction and fulfillment is when *we* create it—accomplish it. When I think of the many years I used "being dumb" as an excuse not to do this or to be that—oh well! At least *today* I know better: I think of being responsible as being free!

We are so magnificent and know not what we are! Let's be willing to look, to uncover what keeps us locked up in this illusion of low self worth.

Low Self Worth Worksheet

How does this distraction keep you from being who you are and from doing what you really want to do?

What actions are you willing to take to be who you are and to do what you really want to do?

onward . . .

Onward and Upward

My son, Christopher, asked, "Will you include what distractions can produce?" Every distraction contains within it a possibility, an opportunity, a catalyst for change, every single one—those we have chosen and those we have been given that have us avoiding what we really want to do and who we are.

Because we are alive we think we are conscious. And on a medical level we certainly are. But there are other levels of consciousness and raising these levels is what each of us really wants whether or not we realize it. Being more and more conscious on these levels will find us making the choices that will bring us the desired results of our hearts. It's really not complicated (as our egos like to portray)! I could write another book on the subject of consciousness. Webster defines it as "awareness/perception of an inward psychological or spiritual fact; intuitively perceived knowledge of something in one's inner self; mind in the broadest possible sense: something in nature that is distinguished from the physical."

So to be awake to what we are feeling, thinking, hearing, seeing, saying, doing, not doing, being or not being will produce more love of self and others. It will enable us to recognize a distraction when it appears. Wanting to live consciously comes from being interested, curious, concerned and possessing a deep desire to have a full/rich life.

I haven't used the word "God" because it's so much more than just a word—so many millions of interpretations, so immense yet so very personal. Since I believe that God is all there is, God was not left out of this book.

So, dear reader, onward and upward on your precious journey. Allow everything that shows up in your life to move you into being who you are and doing what you really want to do.

(All for now!)

Postscript

On September 11, 2001 I had two chapters of this book left to write. (Did I mention "distractions"?) The priority for me was to honor my feelings. I was in grief and depression for about three weeks—totally immobile! Still unable to understand such utter darkness, I have accepted it. Flying our own colors to remind me of freedom has helped. Who America is, is a stand for freedom. I need to be aware of my stand for freedom. Am I a stand for freedom? What really is freedom?

I see tremendous opportunity and possibility coming out of this tragedy. The global unity can produce the end of world hunger, we can lift the veils of women slaves, end the drug traffic, and lift the spirits of suffering children. If we trust, believe, and go to work! Freedom!!

I love these words expressed by the incredible Anne Frank:

> I don't think of all the
> misery
> but of all the beauty
> that still remains.

The Day Our Skies Were Quiet

I wondered what the birds
were saying
When the planes stopped
flying
And the stillness was a
praying
Felt around the world.
Every heart was broken,
every eye a sea of tears.

Darkest evil had just
spoken,
Unveiling its secret scheme
of fears
Onto a sweet September morn
That promised another lively
day.

Today the innocence is gone,
But chins are up, eyes are clear
As hearts grow big and minds
go deep
To understand, be free of fear
And live again under safe blue skies.

Faith Fayman Strong, September 12, 2001

Acknowledgements

My every thought, every feeling, every spoken word and every creative expression rests on the backs of every one I have ever met, known, loved, disliked, read about, been exposed to, or experienced. I thank you all for the priceless gems that have been a part of my life's building materials.

Having said that, I want to acknowledge specifically those that have supported me in creating this book.

To my oldest son, Barry John Lyerly, who has been my writing coach; to Joyce Lerner, my editor; to my other children: Linda, Christopher, David, Hope Adele and Deborah; to supportive and helpful friends: Jessica, Kay, Andrea, Lau and Kaleta and Charlotte and many others (they know who they are)—a million thanks—and a million more.